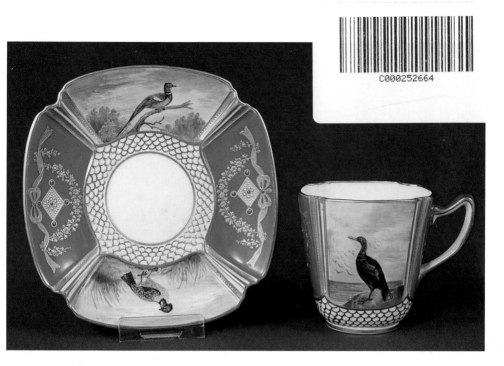

Copeland bone china cup and saucer, Queen Anne shape, c.1884; painting attributed to the artist C. Weaver. (Copeland China Collection)

COPELAND

Vega Wilkinson

A Shire Book

Published in 2000 by Shire Publications Ltd,
Cromwell House, Church Street, Princes Risborough,
Buckinghamshire HP27 9AA, UK.
(Website: www.shirebooks.co.uk)

Copyright © 1994 and 2000 by Vega Wilkinson.
First published 1994 as Shire Album 306.
Second edition with colour illustrations, published in 2000.
ISBN 0 7478 0462 1.
Vega Wilkinson is hereby identified as the author of this
work in accordance with Section 77 of the Copyright,
Designs and Patents Act 1988.

British Library Cataloguing in Publication Data:
Wilkinson, Vega
Copeland. – 2nd ed. – (The Shire book)
1. W.T. Copeland & Sons
2. Pottery – England – 19th century
3. Pottery, England – 20th century
I. Title 738'.0942
ISBN 0 7478 0462 1

Cover: *(Top row, from left to right) Copeland majolica bottle vase of the 1880s (private collection). Parian figure of 1861, 'The Bride'. Spode Copeland bone china model of a magpie, c.1970s. (Bottom row, left to right) Copeland bone china dessert plate, c.1891, Belinda shape, with goldfinch design hand-painted by C. F. Hürten. Plate of c.1851, 'The Tower of Comares', painted by Daniel Lucas Junior.*

ACKNOWLEDGEMENTS
I gratefully acknowledge the advice and support given to me by many people while writing this book. Jean and Spencer Copeland of Trelissick Mansion, Cornwall, gave me their generous hospitality, providing full access to the family archives and supplying many new photographs of pieces from the Copeland China Collection. Harold Holdway, formerly art director for Spode, placed his vast knowledge of Spode and Copeland at my disposal, along with photographs from his archives. Robert Copeland has given freely of his expert knowledge and made available photographs and also material from his book *Spode and Copeland Marks*. Joan Jones, Curator of the Minton Museum, Stoke-on-Trent, gave helpful and sound advice on the preparation of this book. Jack Shaw of Leeds photographed pieces for me and J. Matthews of H. & B. Graeme, Fowey, Cornwall, photographed the Copeland China Collection. Bill Coles photographed pieces from his own collection and that of his wife, and they have kindly allowed their reproduction here. Anne Roberts gave editorial assistance with the manuscript and Jacqueline Fearn has made this book possible. The illustrations on pages 16 and 17 are from the old badge books in the Spode archives, Stoke-on-Trent.

Printed in Malta by Gutenberg Press Limited,
Gudja Road, Tarxien PLA 19, Malta.

Contents

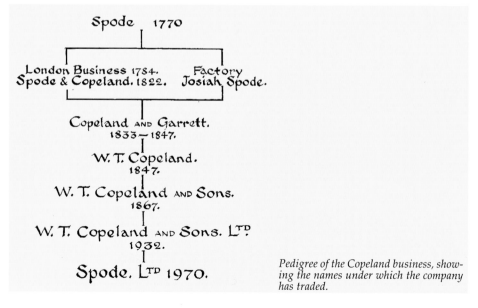

Pedigree of the Copeland business, showing the names under which the company has traded.

Copeland & Garrett, 1833–47

The entrance to the Spode works in Stoke-upon-Trent as it was in the 1880s; drawn in 1993 by Harold Holdway, who worked for W. T. Copeland & Sons Ltd from the 1930s to the 1970s, becoming art director.

In the late eighteenth century Josiah Spode I was the master of a highly successful pottery, aided by his son Josiah II, who ran the London showroom and warehouse with William Copeland, who had joined the firm in 1784. In 1797, after his father's death, Josiah II returned to Stoke-upon-Trent to run the Spode works.

The art of under-glaze printing in blue had been the keystone of his father's success. Now Josiah II perfected the making of bone china, finding a ready market for it in his London showroom, where he had sent his son William to learn the business with William Copeland.

William Spode retired from the business in December 1811 and an agreement was signed, giving Josiah II a quarter share and Copeland three-quarters. In 1826 William Copeland died and his shares in the London business, trading from Portugal House, Lincoln's Inn Fields, passed to his only son, William Taylor Copeland (1797-1868), who had become a partner in the firm. He and Josiah II entered into a seven-year partnership.

However, Josiah II died in 1827, followed soon afterwards by his son Josiah III. The remaining members of the family decided to sell the whole business, and in 1833 it was bought by William Taylor Copeland.

Copeland then took Thomas Garrett into partnership, sending him to Stoke to run the factory. Garrett had been a traveller for the firm for many years and was highly regarded by the Copeland family. The

China goblet and salver (left) showing the arms adopted by Thomas Garrett and made to celebrate the Copeland &Garrett partnership in 1833 and (below) the inscription on the base of the salver. (Copeland China Collection)

signing of the partnership agreement in 1834 was celebrated by the roasting of an ox, the bones of which were used in the production of two punchbowls, two salvers and two goblets. A salver and a goblet were given to each partner and decorated with their coat of arms. The punchbowl made for the Talbot Inn, Stoke-upon-Trent, is displayed at the Spode Museum in the city and the other, made for the Wheatsheaf Inn, Stoke, and both salvers and goblets are in the Copeland China Collection, Trelissick, Cornwall.

Copeland & Garrett inherited from the Spodes an excellent art department run by Thomas Battam, who had become art director in 1835. An artist of great merit, Battam had been trained in his father's decorating business in Gough Street, London, and he was responsible for the Etruscan designs of this period. It was he who later recognised that the new body called Statuary Porcelain, better known as Parian, would

Right: Bone china punchbowl, 1833; made for the Wheatsheaf Inn, next to the Spode works in Stoke-upon-Trent, at the suggestion of the landlord, Thomas Grocott.

Left: Copeland & Garrett bone china donkey ornament, dating from about the 1840s. This model was also produced in Parian. (Copeland China Collection)

5

Above: Copeland & Garrett Parian Beauvais jug c.1830s. These jugs were made in different sizes.

Right: 'Narcissus', modelled by E. B. Stephens, based on the sculpture by John Gibson, and executed in Statuary Porcelain for the Art Union of London, 1844.

become very popular. Parian was used to recreate famous sculptures of the day in a much reduced size.

When the well-known sculptor John Gibson RA (1790–1866), accompanied by a group of other sculptors and representatives of the Art Union of London, visited the Spode works in 1844, he pronounced Parian 'the next best material to marble' and agreed to allow his sculpture 'Narcissus' to be used as a model. A perfect replica of the original was modelled by the sculptor E. B. Stephens but Victorian prudery necessitated the addition of a fig-leaf in the appropriate place; Stephens requested, as part of his fee, the only figure which was produced unadorned!

In 1846 the Art Union of London, whose aim was to promote all forms of art, commissioned fifty statues of Narcissus to be offered as prizes to their subscribers. These proved very popular. As Art Unions sprang up in many of the major cities of England and Scotland, Copelands received commissions from them. The range of Parian products extended to more figures, busts of famous people, animals and groups and was highly successful. Battam's faith in the product had been well founded.

Copeland & Garrett ware changed to meet changing fashion, moving away from the classical purity of the Georgian era. Just as early Victorian furniture became more robust, with more carved ornamentation, so too Copeland & Garrett ware became much more ornate, with an enormous increase in the range of products.

Tiles were a popular line at this time, many of them incorporating the designs used on tableware. Others illustrated scenes from Shakespeare. Tiled panels were used widely in the entrance halls of houses, in restaurants and shops and in fireplace surrounds of varying

Above: *Copeland coloured Parian elephant, 'Jumbo', from the Barnum circus, 1880s. (Copeland China Collection)*

Right: *Copeland decorated Parian figure, 'Robinette', 1880s. (Copeland China Collection)*

Copeland transfer-printed hand-painted tile of Malvolio, one of a set of tiles depicting scenes and characters from Shakespeare, in the Spode Museum, Stoke-on-Trent. Width 203 mm.

shapes. China slabs of all sizes were set into tabletops and into furniture.

The well-equipped kitchen of an affluent home would have a range of bowls, basins and jugs for every culinary use, including moulds for jellies, aspics and meat and fish pastes. Here too were the plates and dishes for the servants' meals, the tableware for the senior servants being more decorative than that of the lower staff.

Great quantities of ware were essential, for these were still the days of enormous breakfasts, luncheons, and afternoon teas to bridge the gap before dinner. Later, in the evening, suppers were laid out to await

7

(Right) Spode sucrier, c.1815, 70 mm. (Left) Copeland & Garrett sucrier, c.1845, pattern number 5369, 121 mm.

those members of the family who had been to the theatre, opera or one of the many gentlemen's clubs.

In the dining room the potter's art was displayed in the flatware and hollow-ware laid out on the gleaming mahogany table and sideboards, ranging from bone china placecards and menu holders to huge soup tureens. Dessert services were hand-painted and decorated with botanical studies or landscapes, reflecting the owner's interests and providing a topic for dinner-table conversation. These services would include tall, medium and low comports and large ice pails, all superbly painted and gilded.

The drawing room held many objects to delight the eye: vases large and small, spill vases, candle holders and Parian figures or groups. Copeland & Garrett could even provide china door plates with door knobs to match. In the library, study and smoking rooms gentlemen were catered for with ashtrays and tobacco jars.

Copeland & Garrett bone china tea cups and saucer, hand-painted, c.1840s. The pattern is typical of the period.

Bedrooms were not forgotten. Here were bedside candle holders and ornaments for the mantelshelf, while on the washstand there were toilet sets comprising ewers and bowls, soap dishes and tooth mugs and, hidden discreetly in a cupboard or under the bed, were the matching chamber pot and lidded slop pail.

The Victorian passion for collecting plants for the garden and conservatory resulted in yet another range of goods, from garden pots and jardinières to garden seats. In November 1846 the *Art Union*

Above left: *Copeland & Garrett dessert plate, c.1843; pattern number 6903; named on the reverse* LAKE URI. *Artist unknown.*

Above right: *Copeland & Garrett bone china candle snuffers and stand, c.1840. (Copeland China Collection)*

magazine reported: 'Messrs Copeland & Garrett have taken the neglected flower pot under their essential guardianship. Humble as its fate had been hitherto, they have seen that it is worthy and susceptible of ornamentation and they have thus commenced to bring our conservatories and green houses within the range of decorative art.'

Under-glaze blue-printed earthenware, decorated with Spode patterns such as Willow, Blue Italian and Geranium, not only were still popular in Britain but sold well in Europe, the United States and Canada. In 1835

Above: *Pair of Copeland & Garrett vases encrusted with lilies of the valley, c.1840s. (Copeland China Collection)*

Left: *Copeland & Garrett bone china door furniture, c.1840s; painting attributed to W. Ball. (Copeland China Collection)*

Flower pots and other garden wares by Copeland & Garrett, from the Art Union magazine, November 1846.

Copeland & Garrett negotiated a contract with the Hudson Bay Company to be their sole suppliers of earthenware. Excavations on their trading-post sites have shown that 109 different patterns were ordered. This contract lasted until the 1870s.

Floral designs drawn from nature were popular at home and abroad, being adaptable to both tableware and ornaments. On the more expensive services the botanical name of the flower was painted on the reverse of the piece. Different species of birds were also depicted, and landscapes were fashionable, often of ruined castles and Roman antiquities copied from the travel books and engravings of the period.

In 1829 William Taylor Copeland had become an alderman for the Bishopsgate ward in the Corporation of the City of London. His political standing reached its peak in 1835, when he became Lord Mayor of London. A full range of high-quality Copeland & Garrett goods, including earthenware, bone china, majolica and Parian, was always on display in the London showroom, and William Taylor Copeland's many influential friends came to order special sumptuous services for their homes.

A reporter on the 1843 *Penny Magazine,* describing a day in the Staffordshire Potteries, wrote: 'The manufactory was the largest in the district, employing 1000 hands and having 120 separate workshops.'

Artists at Copeland & Garrett were still influenced by the work of Henry Daniel, the enameller, who had worked with Josiah Spode II in the early nineteenth century. Daniel was responsible for fine hand-painted designs and, although he left to start his own business in 1822, his designs continued to be popular throughout the Copeland & Garrett period and into the 1880s.

In 1847 the partnership between William Taylor Copeland and Thomas Garrett was dissolved. Copeland continued trading but under his name alone, W. T. Copeland.

William Taylor Copeland (1797–1868), who bought the Spode business in 1833. This portrait, by Mrs Charles Pearson, was painted in 1835, when Copeland was Lord Mayor of London.

The mid Victorian period: W. T. Copeland, 1847–67

For the next twenty years Alderman Copeland ran the firm alone, continuing to produce a full range of products and now trading from 160 New Bond Street, London.

When in 1850 Prince Albert appointed a Royal Commission to promote the First International Exhibition, Alderman Copeland was chosen as a commissioner to represent the pottery industry. The International Exhibition of All Nations, known as the Great Exhibition, held in Hyde Park, London, in 1851 provided the pottery industry with the first opportunity to see the work of the famous factories of Sèvres, Meissen and Dresden and to exhibit their own finest ware. Copelands took Parian pieces, large and small, finely painted vases, earthenware and bone china dessert services and their new product Jewelled Porcelain, designed by William Henry Goss. He became their chief artist in 1857 but left in 1858 after a disagreement with Thomas Battam and started his own pottery.

The panel of experts reported: 'Mr Copeland shows a large assortment of plates and other articles of ornamental porcelain, the flower painting and gilding of many of them are very good; and especially in the centering of the plates, much taste is observable in the arrangement of the pattern. Some large vases of Etruscan shape and decoration are most handsome. Mr Copeland has also some articles in which the effect

Two Copeland bone china pieces from the so-called Shah's Service, 1857, probably commissioned by Queen Victoria as a gift for Napoleon III and later acquired by the Shah of Persia. (Left) Comport and stand with modelled lions rampant, bearing the Royal Arms of the United Kingdom; heraldic work by William Henry Goss; height 406 mm. (Below) Oblong footed comport, the continental scene attributed to Daniel Lucas Junior.

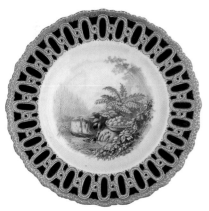

Pierced dessert plate, Windsor shape, with raised and chased gold border, painted by C. F. Hürten, c.1880s. A detail of the decoration, including Hürten's signature, is shown to the right.

of inlaid pearls and other jewels is rendered with considerable success.'

The exhibits of the state-aided factories of Sèvres and Meissen were superb, the hand-painted floral decoration being of exceptional quality. After the Exhibition Alderman Copeland recognised the need to improve the standard of flower painting on his ware, so that it could compete more favourably with Sèvres and Meissen. In Paris he saw the work of Charles Ferdinand Hürten (1820–1901), an established German artist, noted for his flower painting, who had been trained at the Cologne School of Art and had worked for Sèvres. In 1858 Copeland persuaded him to come to the Spode works on a salary of £320 per annum. At this time he was the only artist to have his own studio and to be allowed to paint freely on any type of ware. In addition he was allowed to sign his work, which was in constant demand and commanded a high price. Hürten's unique artistry set a standard which all other artists throughout the industry tried to attain.

One of the finest examples of Hürten's work is the dessert and tea service commissioned by the Prince of Wales on the occasion of his marriage in 1863. The service consisted of 196 pieces and took three years to complete. Hürten painted orange blossom, fruit and flowers on the four panels in the border of the dessert plates.

Copelands produced many fine bone china pieces decorated with landscapes. Their leading artist in this field was Daniel Lucas Junior, son of the Derby artist. He was employed by Copelands, it is thought, on a freelance basis, between the 1850s and the 1870s.

The special order books in the Spode archives record, on 25th September 1857, a special service known now as the Shah's Service because it was later bought by the Shah of Persia, although the date of purchase is not known. It is thought that it was

Bone china festoon-embossed dessert plate from the service commissioned by the Prince of Wales in 1863; painted by C. F. Hürten; 225 mm. (Spode Museum)

Above left: *Copeland bone china tray, c.1880, with embossed basket-woven sides, painted with a group of wild flowers and grasses; signed C. F. Hürten; length 254 mm.*

Above right: *Earthenware Chelsea shape dessert plate, c.1860s. (Copeland China Collection)*

commissioned by Queen Victoria as a present for Napoleon III. The service was decorated with named landscapes attributed to Daniel Lucas Junior. One comport was supported by three lions rampant bearing shields, having the Royal Arms of the United Kingdom and the profile heads of Queen Victoria and Prince Albert in raised gold. The other comport held the Napoleonic arms and the profile heads of the Empress Eugènie and Napoleon III. Every piece has a simulated jewelled border, the design of which is attributed to Goss. The borders were moulded with tiny indentations, which were painted with gold, and then coloured pieces of glass were inserted into them to simulate jewels.

The work of Thomas Battam's team of highly skilled artists and gilders was seen on Copeland exhibits at other international exhibitions, held in London, Paris and Vienna.

Copelands had secured a profitable order for the 1862 London exhibition, supplying 10,000 earthenware plates, 1000 earthenware tureens, 10,000 china coffee cups and 5000 teacups as well as 3000 jugs for milk and cream. Their exhibition of special pieces was again highly praised.

These exhibitions led to orders for sumptuous services not only from the visiting public but also from the famous china showrooms such as Thomas Goode & Company of South Audley Street, London, who often commissioned Copeland's finest work.

Copeland Parian bottle vase, c.1860s, decorated by the French artist Charles Grègoire, noted for his fine rose paintings.

13

Other members of the team of artists were Richard (?) Greatbatch, John (?) Plant, William Ball and William Birbeck. Greatbatch was a floral artist of the highest merit. His studies of flowers were very popular but unfortunately the special order books do not give his initials. They do, however, show 'R. Greatbatch' as an artist gilder who executed complicated designs of gilding that enhanced pieces sent to the Great Exhibition of 1851. Plant painted landscapes. Ball designed and painted many fine pieces, and his floral studies were featured on ceramic tiles used on table tops and other furniture. Birbeck joined the team in the early 1860s, painting landscapes. He signed his work.

Except for Hürten, all artists and gilders at Copelands were paid for each piece they painted, the rate being agreed

Above: Copeland bone china large ornamental vase and cover; Chatsworth shape; painting attributed to Charles Weaver Senior, c.1860s. (Copeland China Collection)

Right: Copeland earthenware water bottle, stand and cover; pattern number D 758, c.1857; impressed COPELAND. *It is rare to find the water bottle complete with stand and cover.*

Copeland bone china dessert plate, Windsor shape, c.1861. The hand-painted bird in the centre is a hoopoe. (Private collection)

with the foreman. The special order books show varying rates, from 2s 6d to 10s 6d for a landscape painting, depending on the complexity of the painting or gilding. It was not uncommon for two artists to paint on the same piece at differing rates. Their wages depended upon the skill and speed with which they worked, their output being counted at the end of each day. Artists soon learnt the knack of negotiating for the best price, keeping it a closely guarded secret from their colleagues.

During the mid Victorian period Copelands, although continuing to produce special pieces for the exhibitions, did not neglect their established customers and produced fine earthenware, decorated with popular blue and white patterns, kitchen and toilet wares and fine bone china dinner, tea and coffee services of exceptional quality.

In 1866 the firm was appointed china and glass manufacturers to HRH the Prince of Wales. The following year Alderman Copeland took his four sons into partnership with him. His eldest son, William Fowler Mountford Copeland, became the senior partner, whilst Alfred James Copeland ran the London showroom and Edward Capper Copeland and Richard Pirie Copeland ran the Spode works in Stoke-upon-Trent, Staffordshire. The firm now traded as W. T. Copeland & Sons.

Copeland bowl and jug in crown body earthenware with blue transfer-printed design from the 1870s. It is marked 'COPELAND late SPODE' and has the crown body impressed mark with the year '73' (for 1873). Crown body is a white earthenware developed between 1847 and 1855; pieces are marked on the reverse with an impressed crown.

W. T. Copeland & Sons, 1868–1913

In 1868 Alderman Copeland died suddenly. His sons continued to run the business.

During the nineteenth century many organisations ordered earthenware and china tableware on which their official coat of arms or badge would be incorporated in the design. Creating new badges, crests and logos kept the engraving and transfer departments at the Spode works very busy throughout this period. Badges were simple and printed in a choice of colours but those incorporating armorial bearings designed for the livery and shipping companies were more ornate.

Copeland design for a regimental china dessert plate incorporating the badge of the 28th South Gloucestershire Regiment. The tableware was invoiced on 3rd September 1868.

Regiments serving at home and abroad ordered large dinner services. Those for the officers' mess were made of bone china, highly gilded and decorated, whilst the sergeants' mess had earthenware with a simpler design and badge. As regiments amalgamated, new badges were created and more services ordered. The Indian Army was a valued customer. Wherever the army served Copeland ware went too!

Earthenware and china tableware decorated with the company's

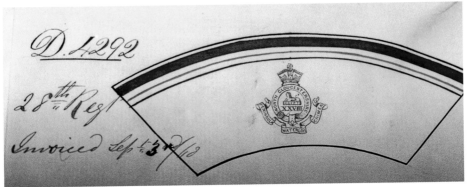

Designs incorporating the badges of (far left) the Commissioners of Irish Lights and (near left) the 43rd Regiment of Bengal Native Infantry.

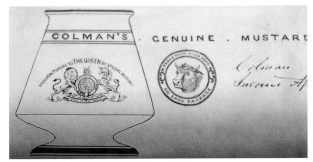

Backstamp for Colman's mustard showing the Colman's trademark, a bull's head.

badge were ordered in large quantities by railway companies for use in the dining cars on trains and refreshment rooms on station platforms. The badge and crest books in the Spode archives record that eating houses and inns ordered suitable badges on their tableware, serving as an attractive form of advertising.

Mr Colman, the maker of Colman's mustard, of 108 Cannon Street, London, had two backstamps, one with his trademark, a bull's head, the other comprising instructions on how to mix the mustard.

Merchants who specialised in selling potions and ointments ordered earthenware pots with their special badge on the lid, like Mr Ross of Number 119, Bishops Gate Within London, who sold 'Genuine Bear's

Copeland bone china Gordon tray, c.1873, commissioned by the retailer William Savage of Winchester, and decorated with the Trusty Servant pattern.

Above left: *Copeland bone china cup and stand, Huth Tea Tazza shape, marked with the Copeland crossed Cs, c.1879. (Private collection)*

Above right: *Copeland bone china tea plate, cup and saucer; pattern number D7015, c.1880. (Private collection)*

Left: *Copeland earthenware lidded jug, classical design, c.1890s. (Private collection)*

Grease', whilst William Fox of Number 2, Finch Lane, Cornhill, London, had put on his Botanical shaving cream pot, selling at 2s 6d, that his establishment was 'patronised by the English and Continental nobility'.

Parian continued to be popular into the twentieth century. Some Copeland Parian figures were delicately coloured or picked out in gold. Parian plates and small bowls and even cups and saucers were made. Small cherubs in Parian on china special dessert services enhanced the beauty of the piece. Models of the celebrities of the day continued to be produced and in 1871 the Art Union of London commissioned Copelands to produce a bust of Queen Victoria's daughter Princess Louise from an original sculpture by Mary Thorneycroft.

A new range of stoneware was introduced in the late 1880s. Jugs and bowls with a blue or green background, decorated with sprigged designs of hunting scenes or ladies in flowing robes known as 'Houris', were produced. These were so successful that teapots, sugar bowls and milk jugs were added to the range.

In 1887, the year of Queen Victoria's Golden Jubilee, Copelands added commemorative jugs, bowls

Far left: *Copeland Parian ornament impressed* COPELAND, *c.1880s.*

Left: *Parian statue of Florence Nightingale with the mark* COPELAND *impressed on the base and* T. HILARY BONHAM CARTER, *c.1863. (Copeland China Collection)*

Above: *Copeland bone china cup and saucer, painted and signed by Arthur Perry, c.1900s. The service was commissioned by Tiffany of New York. The colour was very popular in America.*

Above: *Copeland majolica bottle vase of the 1880s. Although Copeland did produce a range of majolica ware, examples are hard to find. This one shows the brilliance of the colours. (Private collection)*

Above: *Copeland crown body earthenware plate, c.1884; an unusual design, printed* SILVESTER *on the reverse. (Private collection)*

Right: *Large earthenware Copeland plate, c.1880, painted and signed by Lucien Besche.*

and teapots in an attractive green. Royal weddings, coronations and jubilees were always good for trade in the Potteries.

Although Copelands were still receiving orders and commissions directly from retail houses who supplied royalty and the aristocracy, they found that maintaining the showroom at 160 New Bond Street was becoming too expensive. Times were changing and the demand for highly specialised hand-painted ware was declining. Copelands were now selling exclusive ranges of their goods to the big departmental stores like Harrods of Knightsbridge and Tiffany of New York and in 1881 the showroom was moved to rented accommodation at 12 Charterhouse Street, London.

Above: *Copeland earthenware sweetmeat dish, popular in the 1870s. The design was used on all shapes of ware attributed to the art director Thomas Battam. (Copeland China Collection)*

Right: *Copeland earthenware jug, impressed* COPELAND, *c.1900s; sprigged ware with rugby scenes. (Private collection)*

The Spode works in Staffordshire had expanded and was totally self-sufficient. It made its own bricks for repairing old bottle ovens, erecting new ones and building new potting shops. The site contained a caskmakers' shop for making the casks in which the finished ware was dispatched, a blacksmiths' forge and a joiners' shop.

After the death of Thomas Battam in 1868 the art department was run for a short time by George Eyre but in the early 1870s Robert Frederick Abraham was appointed as art director. Abraham had been trained in Antwerp and Paris and was a fine figure painter. Under his direction Copelands produced some of their finest ware for the Paris Exhibition of 1889. The complete display was bought by Thomas Goode & Company of London.

The *Staffordshire Advertiser* in 1889 reported: 'Messrs Copeland's collection is in every respect – novelty, variety, technical skill and artistic merit – worthy of their historic reputation.'

One of the main exhibits was the Mecklenburg Service. Thomas Goode & Company had commissioned Copelands to produce an exact replica of a service made by the Chelsea factory in 1763. It was called

Copeland bone china tureen and stand, c.1889; replica of the Mecklenburg Service decorated with exotic birds.

Above left: *Copeland bone china dessert plate, Belinda shape, c.1891, hand-painted by Charles Ferdinand Hürten and initialled 'C. F. H.'. This goldfinch is a rare example of a bird painting by him.*

Above right: *Copeland earthenware plaque, 1883, painted and signed by C. J. Weaver. A pleasant study of a common or European partridge with her chicks at the edge of a cornfield.*

the Mecklenburg because the original service was purchased by Queen Charlotte as a present to her brother, Duke Adolphus Frederick IV of Mecklenburg-Strelitz. The modelling alone cost £400.

At this exhibition Hürten's work was again highly praised. The reporter, after describing other Copeland exhibits, continues: 'It is in sharp contrast to turn from these to a collection of slabs and plaques enriched with the ever welcome pencil of Mr Hürten, a veteran (if he will excuse our saying so) whose artist's eye is not dimmed nor his natural force abated.'

Abraham had many talented artists under his supervision, and many were now allowed to sign their names. In 1897 Charles Brough, painting fish and other subjects, was chosen to demonstrate the art of ceramic painting to the Princess of Wales when she visited the Spode works. Other notable artists were Thomas Sadler, painting roses; L. Rivers, who painted both flowers and fish; William Birbeck, painting fine landscapes; William Yale, who painted landscapes on plaques; and

Below left: *Copeland earthenware hot water kettle marked* SPODE COPELAND ENGLAND, *c.1890s.*

Below right: *Copeland dessert plate, earthenware B body, Belinda shape, marked '2/755', c.1877; a good floral design; impressed* COPELAND.

Above left: *Copeland earthenware large claret jug, deco-*
rated with the transfer-printed scene 'Going to the Derby',
c.1868. (Copeland China Collection)

Above right: *Copeland earthenware jug, impressed*
COPELAND, *c.1900, unusual sprigged design and engine-*
turned decoration. (Private collection)

Left: *Copeland bone china plaque, c.1884. This fine piece*
was painted and signed by H. C. Lea after Tadema.
(Copeland China Collection)

Below left: *A pair of earthenware vases by Copeland,*
c.1870: the painting is a rare and fine example of the work
of William Yale. (Copeland China Collection)

Below right: *Copeland bone china dessert plate, Richelieu*
shape; 'Lady Teazle, The School for Scandal', painted by
Samuel Alcock, c.1889. (Spode Museum)

Left: *Copeland coloured Parian menu holder, 'the Hooded Rat', c.1880s. (Copeland China Collection)*

Right: *Copeland bone china milk churn with cat handle, c.1880s. This design was very popular and made in different sizes, and the cat handle varied in colour. (Copeland China Collection)*

Right: *Copeland bone china sugar pot, c.1874, decorated with a Chinese design in unusual colours. (Copeland China Collection)*

Below left: *Copeland bone china white tall comport with pierced rim. This design was very popular during the 1900s. (Copeland China Collection)*

Below right: *Copeland bone china trinket pot, c.1910, hand-painted and signed by Arthur Perry. (Copeland China Collection)*

Above left: *China souvenir cup commemorating the late King Edward VII, illustrated in an old marketing leaflet.*

Above right: *China coupe shape dessert plate, 1890s, painted by Thomas Sadler.*

Left: *Copeland bone china vase, c.1890, decorated in the Japanese Imari style; height 152 mm.*

Samuel Alcock, the only artist employed at Copelands on a freelance basis who earned over £300 per year. He worked from his home near the Spode works. The undecorated pieces were taken to him on a handcart with the ceramic colours, brushes and sketching paper. A temperamental man, he had continual arguments with Richard Pirie Copeland. Alcock created a market for dessert services decorated with ladies of fashion, ladies in court costume and heads in the style of Gainsborough, as well as scenes from Shakespeare and Sheridan. His pieces, ordered by Thomas Goode & Company of London and Tiffany of New York, were sold for very high prices before he had completed them.

Copeland bone china dessert plate, Belinda shape, c.1883. The raised gilding was originally designed by Charles Brayford. (Private collection)

Copeland china Madras shape dessert plate with pierced, raised and chased gold border; Shakespearian scene painted by Samuel Alcock, c.1880s.

Abraham's art department employed not only many skilled artists and gilders but also fine painters and paintresses. The market for fine hand-painted and highly gilded services was dwindling but Copelands had anticipated market trends. Transfer designs, filled in skilfully by painters and paintresses on both earthenware and china, sold well. Gold transfer-printed tea and coffee services were particularly attractive. Old Spode pattern books still provided Copeland designers with inspiration. Catalogues which have survived show the many shapes and patterns which were available.

On the death of Richard Pirie Copeland in 1913, the business passed to his two sons, Richard Ronald John Copeland and Alfred Gresham Copeland.

The twentieth century:
W. T. Copeland & Sons Ltd

By the early twentieth century the art department had become much smaller. Hand-painted dessert services were too expensive to produce. The average home bought services decorated with fine transfer-printed designed patterns known as print and enamel. Only a few artists were now employed. Arthur Perry became well-known for painting landscapes, fish and game, whilst Harry Hammersley's floral studies, such as Gainsborough pattern, following the traditional Spode practice of creating a different floral study for each plate, were always in demand. Charles Deaville, the chief gilder, ran a large department producing fine hand-gilded or jewelled borders on dessert services: over ten gilders' names are recorded in the special order books. These artists and their colleagues executed the orders still received for sumptuous services.

Bone china tea and coffee sets sold well, but much of Copeland's output was in earthenware. Spode's blue and white patterns on tea and dinner ware were now being

Above: China Marco shape card bowl, the scene 'Dinant' painted by Arthur Perry, c.1900s. (Spode Museum)

Below: Group of earthenware decorated with Gainsborough pattern, designed by Harry Hammersley, c.1930s.

Copeland earthenware plate, c.1928, registered number 730502, pattern number 2/8470. This pattern was called New Japan. (Private collection)

supplied in different colours: for example, Germany ordered Tower pattern in blue and pink. Hospitals, railways, regiments and airlines continued to order tea and dinner ware on which their special badge or crest was printed.

Although trade fluctuated in the period after the First World War, Copelands retained their market share. Sydney Thompson had been appointed sole agent for the United States of America. He marketed the ware as 'Spode', using 'Spode' in red as his logo, emphasising quality and hand craftsmanship and selling a variety of designs derived from old Spode patterns. In 1924 two new companies were formed: Copeland & Thompson Inc, New York, and Copeland & Duncan Ltd, Toronto, Canada.

Thomas Hassall had been appointed art director in 1912, having served his apprenticeship at Copelands as a floral artist. Recognising the market's demand for Spode-derived patterns, he produced in 1931 Chinese Rose pattern on earthenware, based on Spode's India pattern; it proved so popular that in 1939 it was introduced on bone china.

As a contrast, a pattern known as The Hunt, based on the sketches of J. F. Herring (1795–1865), the coachman artist, was designed and sold well in Britain and in Europe. Originally it was called Herring's Hunting

Group of earthenware decorated with Chinese Rose pattern, 1930s.

27

China dessert plates decorated with The Hunt pattern, 1930s. (Copeland China Collection)

Above left: *Copeland Spode ashtray; an example of the Art Deco style design called Onyx, c.1932.*

Above right: *The polar bear designed by Eric Olsen, made by Copeland, c.1930s, marked 'Velamour' and impressed with the shape number K447. Olsen also designed other animals, and these are very collectable today.*

pattern but the name was changed because German customers could not see how the herring, a fish, was associated with English hunting scenes.

In 1932 Copelands bought the Longton firm Jackson & Gosling, which made Grosvenor China, from Arthur Edward (Ted) Hewitt, who became a member of the board of Copelands, which now traded as W. T. Copeland & Sons Ltd. Hewitt was responsible for modernising the Spode works to increase production, building new tunnel ovens fired first by gas, later by electricity, and reorganising the factory layout.

Fashion was again changing. In Britain the Art Deco style of geometric and jazzy designs in bright harsh colours on exciting new shapes was popular. Ted Hewitt persuaded the modeller Eric Olsen to come to Copelands from Wedgwood; his designs of animals, vases of varying shapes and bowls in the new bodies of Green Jade and Velamour, an ivory matt glaze, were a great success. Advertisements for Royal Jade

Left: *Copeland bone china thrush, c.1914. (Private collection)*

Right: *Copeland earthenware Toby jug, c.1930s. These jugs were produced in a variety of different colours and designs and were very popular in the 1930s.*

ware claimed: 'The shapes have been thought out for ease of holding and cleaning, the gentle green is restrained and ever welcoming. Although so inexpensive, the ware is made from precisely the same earthenware body and glaze for the dearer Spode ware. It is hard and strong and stands up resolutely to knocks and chipping.'

Copeland designs of this period were modernistic rather than Art Deco. Banded patterns, with simple lines of shaded colours and silver lustre following the shape of the ware, were produced and sold well on the home market. Agnes Pinder Davis, a London design consultant, was employed for a short time, producing amongst others the pattern Country Souvenir.

Ronald Copeland had always promoted Copelands as a traditional tableware house but, although he disapproved of the new trend in fashion, he had designed Autumn pattern on earthenware and reluctantly approved the modernistic patterns. Gresham Copeland continued to ensure that the standard of the ware, with whatever design, was exceptionally high.

By the late 1930s Copelands were trading in three very different markets. The United States and Canada rejected the new style, demanding from Copelands the traditional Spode designs which appealed to their customers.

Two Spode Copeland bone china figures from the series called 'Cries of London', 1930s, based on paintings by Francis Wheatley (1747–1801): (left) 'Peas'; (right) 'The Milkmaid'.

Copeland's agent in Europe, August Warnecke, was very successful, continually demanding changes to the patterns. In his Hamburg showroom he displayed complete table settings with cutlery and fine glass on shining dining tables. When members of the company visited him he entertained them at restaurants which used only traditionally designed Copeland-Spode dinner services.

These two markets took two-thirds of the company's output, but the home market demanded change. In 1937 Copelands exhibited at the British Industries Fair. Harold Holdway, who was to become chief designer in 1940, designed one sample plate of Fine Stone ware, with a stylistic bird in the centre. Queen Elizabeth (later the Queen Mother) saw the design and ordered a service. Holdway quickly designed the rest of the service and the pattern was called Queen's Bird.

In 1938 Sydney Thompson of Copeland & Thompson Inc requested a Christmas pattern for the American market, and Harold Holdway

designed Christmas Tree on earthenware. When Thompson saw the design he was not convinced that it would sell in America. To his surprise, his staff were enthusiastic and Copelands were commissioned to produce the design on dinner, tea and coffee services. Later fancy dishes, ashtrays and cigarette boxes were added to the range. Christmas Tree became a best-selling pattern and is still in production.

Oriental influence on design could still be found in new patterns such as The Little Fisherman; the fisherman catches not only fish but butterflies.

During the Second World War Copeland's main task was to produce ware for the export market, as

An earthenware plate showing Christmas Tree pattern.

Group decorated with The Little Fisherman pattern on Fine Stone ware, c.1930s, displayed in the drawing room at Russborough, County Wicklow, Ireland. One of Copeland's best-selling patterns, The Little Fisherman was designed by Harold Holdway, using as source material a book brought from Belgium by Thomas Hassall.

throughout the war the pottery industry was allowed to sell only white undecorated ware to the home market. All decorated ware went for export to bring back to Britain much needed dollars. 'Export or die' was the slogan of the time.

After the war households starved of colour bought Copeland's Flemish Green and English Lavender services, now decorated with modernistic designs. Moondrop was influenced by Celtic design and had a strong

Examples of Copeland utility wares made during the Second World War when decoration of wares for the home market was prohibited. The jug shape is known as Galloway.

line pattern and Montego Bay was designed from actual ferns sent back from the western shore of Jamaica.

Copeland's marketing leaflets showed not only the range of goods available in the patterns but told the story of their inception.

The company now emphasised their association with Josiah Spode and were known as 'W. T. Copeland & Sons Ltd selling Spode'. The ware was expensive but, by marketing it for its quality and hand craftsmanship, they competed with the many other factories which had now abandoned hand-painting because of the cost and were decorating their ware with multicoloured transfers. Copeland's art department had been rebuilt and was now a design studio. Artists were taught there to become designers, to create new shapes for the ware and to adapt their designs to new technology.

In 1956 the management changed. Ronald and Gresham Copeland and Ted Hewitt retired and their sons took charge of the business.

Left: *Spode Copeland bone china service, 1950s. The pattern, Rhododendron, was designed by Harold Holdway. Each piece of the service illustrated a different species. (Private collection)*

Below: *Spode Copeland earthenware teapot, sugar bowl and cream jug decorated with Jacinth pattern, designed by Harold Holdway, c.1950. (Private collection)*

Spencer Copeland became managing director, Robert Copeland sales director and Gordon Hewitt export director.

In 1957 Copelands produced Spode's Fortuna earthenware range with newly designed shapes for vases, bowls and garden pots in Velamour and a combination of Flemish Green and Ivory. In 1960 Copelands were granted the Duke of Edinburgh's award for elegant design for Royal College shape. Persia pattern, designed by David Jackson, is a fine example. Throughout the late 1950s and 1960s Copelands continued to produce bone china, earthenware and stoneware in a wide range of shapes and patterns: bone china on thirteen shapes, earthenware on fifteen shapes, and stoneware on Lowestoft shape. Over four hundred patterns were available. The best-selling patterns were Maritime Rose, Chelsea Gardens and Fleurs-de-Lys on china; Blue Italian, Camilla, Tower, Gainsborough, Chinese Rose and The Hunt on earthenware; Queen's Bird and Fitzhugh on stoneware.

Right: Spode Copeland bone china 'Golden Oriole', c.1950. (Private collection)

Group of bone china, Royal College shape, Persia pattern, designed by David Jackson (1960).

Left: *Spode Copeland china tea plate, c.1960s, Barbecue pattern, designed by Christopher Bolton.*

Below: *Spode Copeland earthenware tea service, 1960s; Tricorn shape, designed by Harold Holdway. The pattern is Wayside Flowers by Christopher Bolton.*

However, the increasing cost of production was causing problems for the company. The American company of Copeland & Thompson, now run by George Thompson, Sydney Thompson's son, was finding Christmas Tree pattern too expensive to sell. He asked Harold Holdway, the art director, if it could be produced more cheaply. Holdway knew the only way to do so was to use lithographs, which were much cheaper than hand decoration. The sample plate produced was so good that, when shown the new Christmas Tree, Thompson could not tell the difference. All new patterns, such as Persia, were produced by this method.

Left and below: *Spode Copeland earthenware mug and tea plate, Pets' Farm pattern, designed by David Jackson, 1960s. (Private collection)*

Left: *Spode Copeland earthenware mug, Cutie Kitten pattern, designed by Christopher Bolton, c.1950.*

For 133 years W. T. Copeland & Sons Ltd had responded to change and were a very successful Staffordshire manufactory, never losing sight of the great achievements of Josiah Spode I and II, and recognising that success depended upon the skill of everyone involved in making, designing and decorating the product.

In 1966 Copelands became part of the Carborundum Group of Companies and in 1970 celebrated the bicentenary of the year when Josiah Spode I had started his own factory. An exhibition was held at the Royal Academy in London. The finest examples of early Spode, Copeland & Garrett and over a hundred years of Copeland pieces were

Above: *Spode bone china model of a pheasant, 1970s, hand-painted with matt finish.*

Right: *Spode Copeland bone china model of a magpie, 1970s, hand-painted, glossy finish.*

displayed. A wide selection of present-day ware completed the exhibition, which showed the history of the company, the changing styles and designs and how the ware was produced. HRH Princess Margaret visited both the exhibition and the Spode works in Stoke-on-Trent. Further celebrations were held at the Goldsmiths' Hall, London, including a banquet attended by HRH Princess Anne.

After two hundred years the circle was completed when the company name changed from W. T. Copeland & Sons Ltd to Spode Ltd.

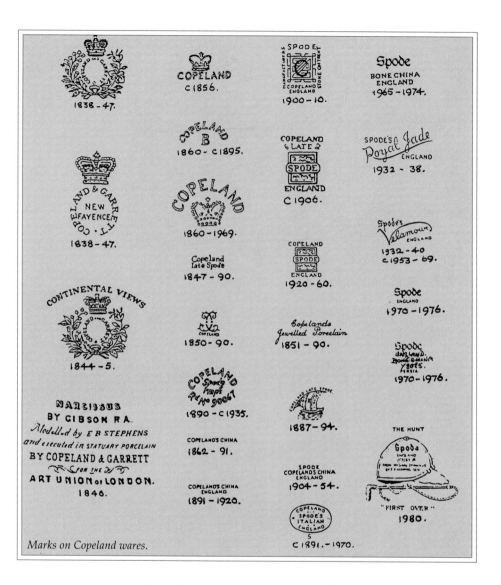

Marks on Copeland wares.

Marks on Copeland wares

COPELAND & GARRETT

The first series of pattern numbers was started by Josiah Spode II, c.1800. Those of Copeland & Garrett begin with 5192 in 1833 and continue to 7747 in 1847. Marks and backstamps of this period were impressed COPELAND & GARRETT, sometimes with LATE SPODE included in the mark. The marks are many and varied, some even bearing the name

Framed china plaque painted (but not signed) by Daniel Lucas Junior, c.1860s.

of the pattern as well. Transfer-printed marks appear in about 1838–9, often having a crown and laurel leaves, and are to be found in pink, green and blue.

W. T. COPELAND

Two sets of pattern numbers were used throughout this period: from pattern number 7747 in 1847 to 9999 in 1857; and also, from 1852, D numbers up to D90, continuing to 1867, when the number D5200 was

Copeland earthenware plaque impressed COPELAND painted and initialled LB (Lucian Besche), 1870s. (Private collection)

Copeland earthenware dish with stand, 1880s; both pieces impressed COPELAND. *The design and colour are both unusual.*

reached. Impressed marks show COPELAND on earthenware, sometimes with B underneath, denoting the type of body of the ware, and sometimes with a crown. Parian is marked with COPELAND impressed in the base of the piece. Those commissioned by the Art Unions have their name and the date. On china, the transfer-printed crossed Cs in green or blue are most common with COPELAND underneath and, from 1862 to 1891, the mark COPELAND'S CHINA.

W. T. COPELAND & SONS

Pattern numbers D5600–D9999 lasted from 1868 to 1874, when a new series of numbers started on china, from 1/504 in 1874 to 1/999 in 1900. Earthenware was numbered from 2/56 in 1874 to 2/4807 in 1900. Impressed marks on both earthenware and china differ very little from those of the mid Victorian era. Printed marks have the addition of ENGLAND added in 1890 to comply with American conditions of trade. The Copeland seal mark or gridiron, incorporating the name SPODE, starting in 1883 and varying in design, was used into the 1960s. From 1887 to 1894 a mark depicting a boat, known as Frank's Boat Mark, is easily recognisable on earthenwares and stonewares. Across the sail is written COPELAND LATE SPODE.

W. T. COPELAND & SONS LTD – SPODE

From 1900 R numbers were introduced on china, reaching R9999 in 1927, followed by Y numbers, reaching Y8155 by 1969. The name of the range of ware was added to the backstamp in 1932–8 Royal Jade and in 1932–40 Fortuna. This ware was reintroduced in 1953–69. From 1970 the printed mark SPODE BONE CHINA ENGLAND became the company's trademark.

Further reading

Copeland, Robert. *Spode and Copeland Marks.* Studio Vista, 1993.

Copeland, R., and Townsend, A. *Spode-Copeland 1733–1983. Potters to the Royal Family since 1803, Stoke-on-Trent.* City of Stoke-on-Trent Museum and Art Gallery, 1983.

Morland, Bill. *Portrait of the Potteries.* Robert Hale, 1978.

Stuart, Denis (editor). *People of the Potteries. A Dictionary of Local Biography*, volume I. Department of Adult Education, University of Keele, 1985.

Wilkinson, Vega. *The Copeland China Collection, Trelissick Mansion, Cornwall.* Mr R. Spencer C. Copeland, 1989.

Wilkinson, Vega. *Spode Copeland Spode 1770–1970.* Antique Collectors' Club, to be published late 2001.

Wood, Christopher. *Victorian Panorama (Paintings of Victorian Life).* Faber & Faber, 1976.

Places to visit

Intending visitors are advised to find out the times of opening and to ascertain that relevant items are on display before making a special journey.

Allen Gallery, Church Street, Alton, Hampshire GU34 1BA. Telephone: 01420 82802. Website: www.hants.gov.uk/museum/allen/index.html

British Museum, Great Russell Street, London WC1B 3DG. Telephone: 020 7636 1555. Website: www.british-museum.ac.uk

Osborne House, East Cowes, Isle of Wight PO32 6JY. Telephone: 01983 200022.

The Potteries Museum and Art Gallery, Bethesda Street, Hanley, Stoke-on-Trent, Staffordshire ST1 3DE. Telephone: 01782 232323. Website: www.stoke.gov.uk/museums

Royal Museum of Scotland, Chambers Street, Edinburgh EH1 1JF. Telephone: 0131 225 7534. Website: www.nms.ac.uk

Spode, Church Street, Stoke-on-Trent, Staffordshire ST4 1BX. Telephone: 01782 744011. Website: www.spode.co.uk

Trelissick, Feock, near Truro, Cornwall TR3 6QL. Telephone: 01872 862248 (Mr R. Spencer C. Copeland). The Copeland China Collection (by appointment only).

Victoria and Albert Museum, Cromwell Road, South Kensington, London SW7 2RL. Telephone: 020 7942 2000. Website: www.vam.ac.uk

Copeland bone china trinket box from a dressing-table set, Richelieu shape, hand-painted, c.1870; marked COPELAND *with crossed Cs. (Copeland China Collection)*